Faunalia

Alice Fulmer

Faunalia

Alice Fulmer

First Published 1 May, 2023 by RITONA

ISBN:979-8-9852028-8-5 (print edition)

RITONA is an imprint of Ritona a.s.b.l.
3 rue de Wormeldange
Rodenbourg, Luxembourg, 6955

Direct queries to distro@abeautifulresistance.com

Visit our website at abeautifulresistance.com

Within

Acknowledgments

Most of these poems have seen the eye of at least one friend or classmate (not mutually exclusive terms) before they were spun into this manuscript. Some of these names include Cole Sabala, Jimmy Vega, Clara Chin, Ricki Hamilton, Sarah Garcia, Damian Wang, Hala, Olivia Bievenue, Kaia Sherry, Caelan Conrad, Lucy Fay, Gardner Dorton, Jos Charles, Justin Zabilski, Michael Parra, Maeve Egílsdóttir and Donna Ghasemni. All my teachers and professors over the years watered so many nourishing seeds for me and my writing. I owe an enormous thank you to my ever patient editor and all around gentleman of the pagan literary world, Rhyd Wildermuth. I would like to express special thanks to my sweethearts Levi Robin and Cassidy for supporting me as a person coming into myself. Lastly but certainly not least, the gods, goddesses, devas, buddhas, bodhisattvas, and spirits who have supplied a constant muse over the last decade.

Warmly,

Alice Grace Fulmer

Spring 2023

Dedicated to the memories of Jordan Taylor Ames (1992-2014), Charles "Charlie" Severino (1996-2021) and Brandon Conley Blaine Curtis (1993-2021)
Et In Arcadia Nos Sumus

"*Faune, Nympharum fugientum amator,*
per meos finis et aprica rura
lenis incedas abeasque parvis
aequus alumnis"

"Faunus, lover of the vanishing nymphs,
May you march through my sunny
and mild homestead, and as you depart:
A little goodwill for all the newborn kids"

Horace, Odes, 3.18

Faunalia Refrains

That time Æneas dropped anchor off the Central Coast
of California in a strait between the Channel Islands,
making a curious water pipe out of a Thracian urn, smoking
the resin of consequences from the Classics in America?
Let's call it Faunalia.

When, after sitting outside their high school Latin class,
those students
of whimsy on rainy days come inside, huddling their desks to
meet
as a hearth and watch the cartoons in perfect meter?
Let's call it Faunalia.

The Tim Burton kid and the Oingo Boingo stan,
a pocketful of band pins between them, in an older, full
size sedan with the Bauhaus blasting?
Let's call it Faunalia.

The sake of spooks and spangles of an aging, Weeping
Willow, just outside a small theme park's
haunted house attraction, with a bronze
satyr statue dancing unprompted and gaily,
direct into once upon a time lovers?
Let's call it Faunalia.

An obscured Roman festival to their god of shepherds,
sex, loud noises and long beards pouring like time's
scrolls and wild dogs galloping vernal
along the humid banks of Tiber Island?
Let's call it Faunalia.

The weight of coffee highs and valleys low,
Dido lips & Sappho thighs, Siouxsie eyes &
hand me down leather, a crossed eye with a
softer gender —
Let's call it Faunalia.

The overzealous cigarette break, far behind
the din of midnight, before the taxes were raised,
forty paces from the toy store halfway out of business,
and the young smoker still hours away from delayed bliss
of a night's sleep purged
through the morning and last sparks of an
afternoon?
Let's call it Faunalia.

That serenity locked in a near dead mall, taut well
in the middle of memories meant to be
ephemeral, hardly tighter than the binding of
cellophane which wrapped the plastic relics
of 1999? The taste of translucent colors, those stained

glass stories of a near digital age, all in one uniform morpheme,
which faded faster than Icarus's virgin voyage to the Sun?
Let's call it Faunalia.

The first zephyrs of spring running, fast off a winter's gone decline
where the first green bangs the onlooker, their
brow busted, so to herbally lobotomize the dregs of
holiday dead and dread?
Let's call it Faunalia.

Cadēns, or Falling

The endemic and imperial decline —your fortune feudal. Clawing
your congested senses with the stringent strength of durians and guavas
on Robin Goodfellow's cheese platter outside an orphanage repossessed
as collateral on a broken bureaucrat's abacus. Never mind the vines.

You live under the sign of a Bad Emperor, after the end of history.
Direct deposit bread and circuses pre-recorded with mythic weight, like
that river banking by the orphanage. Sirens color poverty with repackaged
history in song, "streaming" if you will — never poke your head

out from under their currents. Your rage desalinates down a rivulet and
torrents for an aqueduct, spinning in its guided meditation for wealth
and abundance. There are no priests in tax bombs! They dumped the orphanage,

liquidating the heart into a cashier's check, signed by some electric cadavers'

watermark of nails, after their third serving of pickled iguana. Their same fingers
who scalded out stinky fruit for charity, only when the cameras were dry
to touch, like an oil painting hung in the damp orphanage: a family dinner
with enough to eat. Stability the rhetorical, and well out of your reach,

from this small corner of Tartarus you call 'The Grind.' Grasp for the grapes
for a baton through your smile; slurp the water with a bendy straw and your
FICO score will drop instead, siphoning more fortune down the drain, plug it up
with your hair. You can't drown out the orphans of Capital even when rent's due.

Desert Father

A chaparral road left high and dry, wet
with time travel's perseverance,
beyond hemispheric discrimination.
Holy, holy, holy cactus! Withering with
and beside an elder, rustic roadside lantern
for an old timey saint who used to
be a god. The difference pertinent
only to those who bathe their mantles
in Windex and refuse to dust family
photographs. The saint in question,
bereft of his old, gaudy, purple set of wings
and anthropomorphic titan head now
maintained in icons as a balded,
wilted man. No one remembers his
feast day, unsung like the thorny shadow
of a joshua tree beside the sandy highway

Dear Spirit

let me be as clear as a
metaphysical store's
gem collection:

each dusty thought in a
truffle box of lotus
pedals and bestripe

each one with a fake Rumi
quote, bespoke by a feathered
quill and a bit of sandalwood
crickle-cracking from the swirl of
perfect penmanship, though from one
secretary hand better refined by spiritual
blessings of a million mythological friends...

i would!

but more often, i come home with
sciatica running down my left leg
and a-nagging phone with an app
to reinstall, the growl of a broken
email and a world that's trying to suck
its own dick but can't get past
the bellybutton. the inertia of such

a ruined orgasm dulls the corduroy of a life
devoted to Spirit, like a pair of overalls
without any sort of fun about it. Some days,
I don't wanna be God, unless there's one made
out of potatoes with no pain receptors up or down.
I'll settle for Potato Head as long as I
can smoke the last friendly crumbs of a dead
caterpillar's hookah stash out of the hole where the nose
goes

Cemetery Picnic

On Grandpa Johan's old farm by the criminal creek,
there's turf and trails to the Good Dead
& for the Bad Dead: a mercurial wind!

Way back, the two of us shared some air under a
yellow poplar pair, we'd picnic with his father's
mothers' fathers, by their concrete portraits near our

flannel blanket. Twin hearts grass stained; wrapped in a
textile of stories
twisted, like rotten tooth root tendrils, spread over the
bizarre
economy of lunch. During one of them, he told me for when

"the time came" to simply bury him away
from the sun, and so he was, when Death left. We pushed
him
hand and foot towards the Earth, beside four headstones:

in the dead of the woods, away from the light & the lawns.
So last Father's Day at noon's panic, the reverb of a piccolo
swung through my flowers, like the swoosh of dark, maroon
fairy wings,

above some restless clay, bundled before pre-sliced bread. All
of them
refused to answer my pendulum. Vainly I spoil the
frankincense,
like soaking a skunk in gravy. Bathing the forgotten is a family

chore never finished. The mud of our ilk cracks the anchor
walnuts forgiveness and refusing to sprout in the soil
of smoke and mirrors, acrobats of time's canker sores,

in the wrinkled pockets of two dead and disposable
veterans, their baby sister, some unmarked bones, and then
Grandpa Johan. Not all the fried corn of Mississippi

or the rubber scrotum hanging from the back of cousin
Bill's Ford truck, nor the black & orange of Grindr on
Halloween
in New Orleans will circle back around to relay their needs to
me,

gothic granddaughter, I draw the Seven of Cups and let
the cartomanica wash me over until I am under the artificial
lake nearby,
marooned sea of ivied spirits, peaking to see if the
weathered hearts float

Dispatch, September Third, Twenty Twenty

151 years ago today, Atlanta fell to Union forces
into the dead legacy of another Confederate would-be Atlantis.
Today, it's a wholeass televised comedy, rolling with deadpan punches,
(Pan's not dead)
and deadly obscure in its emotion.
This autumn is kind of like that. There's no red yet,
no orange or yellow in the leaves, so we got half the rainbow yet and hope
that Nature doesn't come for the rest of it.
Like the repo man for your neighbor's Chevy. Things in the sky are dimmer now,
down from burnt summer like a rotisserie chicken at midnight's convenience
store, rolling with Fortune in the grease pan.

Imagine pumpkin spice, but it's poison. This is seasonal catharsis. Now strip away all
that flavor, what we're left with a scene of organisms decaying, no different
than in all of our vestigial holidays, their pointed references bookmarked by guilt's giblets. The autumn accentuates the dismemberment of what is longed to be forgotten.

Autumn is
a crushed insurrection
against the course of life, the resistance brings red to the
green plants and other
breathing beings panting for mutual liberation.

Autumn is a lot like sibling against sibling,
the sentimentality breaking the fall for
the novelty of new dreams. Plenty of old ones too lie
dormant in this space:

- the first day of school
- celebrating the end of Thee Newe Worlde
- smalltown carnivals without the drugs
- Samhain sans the apple blades
- The neutered Labor Day in America and Canada
    - the real one is Beltane's twin
- list of forgotten family recipes
    - what they tasted like to the West Coast tongue

in a Midwestern family reunion

- the bridge across the lake, where
  whispers of Oldsmobiles
  linger like too much nutmeg
- the prospect of new friends

and if should they arrive in an autumnal America,
only to ripen to fall with half the color?

A Father is a Brother

1999, tribulation incoming! Grandma grieves with
a broken neck, to heal slow, given the garnished garlic
of outliving your children. Galloping gallantly,
I come into a room we share, gayly giggling in grace.
She has pheromones from the ghastly & gagged up
old Midwest. Rosewater & golden calves, gromits
of old money. Maybe its Dutch, German, Gaulish, Gomorrahan,
some forgotten pedigree. Her blood is gone from the greed
of love. In the room, I greet Grandma with
a wooden train in hand, gripped with glee, and give a break
from death's constancy. Graves, hers and his, in the good
cupboard, urns anonymous, gray soot grazing the gaunt,
absent man, like his gaze of the globe from his last glass,

Their souls always spread in segues & spirals
a rolling & rustic railway, from station to station.
Now in longing, some souls sag & slip, slumped
in karma. We grieve those, sometimes, who sadly
we never get to know. Patruus the second son,
he's caught up in magnetic tape, silent shots of
time. He's my father's brother sojourning slyly in
the suburbs of Eden. Both sought semblance as siblings

for one fratricidal yolk, simmering, smoking, searing
eggs as familial libations: Salmon with King Solomon's secret
sauce, to grease the wheels of road trips, starving in snake nests
& cracked cobra eggs, hoods of serpents salient from sunny
severance,

my toy and uncle share names: an eponymous elegy,
with an oblong obituary electrically effaced and
straight away from my mind. Escargot emissaries of
fate & fortune alienate us all, as would elections segregated
by a tyrant's touch. Destiny duly emits egregious
dealings, their cards are jet black. Erasure & envy
fill me with words and obligations (emotions empty)
void, vapid, distracting, Every experience
I've had with perfection, even on Ecstasy, elevator
butterfly stomach aches, every and evenly ever
fleeting with the winds of "eternal afterlife",
a family broken up by death in exorcism & exhibition

& sometimes I think of some paternal revelations
guarded I was: in gates of the shepherd's flock in old years
gone by, Grandpa's gold marinated in purgatory's distillery.
Ghosts of great hunger, foodstuffs souls.

Girl, 2040

this interned land is a haunted doll,
with toy gun tyranny and a
snake oil exoskeleton,
but she's thick, the kids say.
Done up like an antique shop icon, but her eyes
are crossed and her porcelain hands, half the color,
come raging, throbbing, cramping in carpal tunnel,
across the appendages of a broken, lonely land.
Those specters are in
their flesh, thirsty with the waves and pants
of a million, ghoulish moans

She's all circuits and spirits
She's America.
and you're out of breath,
your face and hers, half the color

How to Forget Dreams

Coming down with my wings clipped off,
laid on a shore. Shaking in the rumbling dark,
shawled in a shroud of a workman's long unsung
ballad. The moon crowning, a chromosome

in heat. I want to go to a place light
and nothing else.

There's always these dreams at the
beach and I can never feel the sand underneath
my feet. The weight of the breeze, though,
is lighter than stuffed animals and the jet blue,
wavy body in front of me is all that is left from
the Gods' rusty spickets. Straight out the notes of an
anarchist
lawyer, the rules of these realms roll in oil and hay,
sticky and fluffy and unable to be picked apart.
I want to forget the rules, just as pills of white

heavier than the carcass of sleep, than the
sand, tar and the feathers. There's no dirty doctors in these
dreams
either. The apothecary still beseeches a co-pay for the herbal
remedy. But the dryads and druids with the mead
of dandelions text me to hang out when I'm lucky.

They drag away from the water and take me
for an afternoon in Troy, the nice part of town.
Embracing fear is a lot like gazing at your own asshole in the dirty mirror

Forgiving Dreams

Resurrect my springtime sex, garnish it with pheromones.
Springtime floriography spreads its showers and the
humid fog. Silts of soil tremor and bits track under
our feet. Then the moon employs its shadow puppets
to give me another puppet show: a bud pumice and jaundice
with stars for pedals.

I can't remember when last I looked for a four leaf
clover. I forgot about ladybugs and have made peace
with honeybees. Empty easter eggs overturned by
fallacious fortune cookies. They came with takeout
from a Thai place on Sunset, a lusty old boulevard:
all hands and eyes.

The breeze from last night lays in my back pocket and I feel a
draft all through my spine and hairy arms.
Blown out dandelions litter the ground
from optative moods, superstitions towards
a more fruitful time. I'd love to wish an itch
goodbye, forever.

Magic makes the sun shine, and bodies too.
And then there's a call to prayer that makes
me weak in the knees. I submit to the summits,
the crevasse, of the mountains and I hope for

an avalanche. Green grows all over me now. Bring the past to rest, and no empty shores.

A Green Homily

Lord of horns,
        from the grain in the fields
to the calluses on my big toes
        raise me away. Into the mazes
Of rejuvenation, lay your hands
        across the spokes of Fortune's
Wheel, steer the cornfields of time
        with cheer and folly. Let not
sustenance rule the call of the poets
        but a relishment of the details between
the cracks of death and its music of mischievous
        dominion. Run me past the aqueducts,
of misery waft me, sift me, calibrate the
portions of my soul unmotherseen.
Prepare me for a harvest of nines
and nones and knead in me those
moments in meadows and prices
Of pearls. Craft me into a homily
of the Earth and its green spots.

Pacific Time Zone

i. LA

Our moment is out of time like a Babylonian battery.
Today, prosody is an algorithm not for poetry but for
ads and combatants for their blockers. Pinches of faith on the browned spoon,
the smack of tired, greased up hands of the social masses.
Mindfulness the opiate of Lyft drivers & Pilates
coaches and these claims run all staccato
& lost in lists of replies.
Have you checked your Co-Star lately? Mine said:
"Proceed with your story."

These streets are smeared with the sufferin' succotash
of the gig economy, you accumulate capital at any time
if you have the right phone or half-broken car, plus the wrong generation.
We play with the World Trade Center Lego set on the opposite shoreline,
build it up like London bridge one falling, the playground shouting
like the last black crumbs of weed marathoning across, from the
crematory bowl to below the mouthpiece
and today the answers are crystal clear, with the

Steam pressed yoga mats — our gifts of mass production:
retail samadhi! Let the good times roll! With the Hunter
S. Thompson costumes and vintage time and jivin' drugs
with the kids
who want to relive a ~ time ~ in time out of time, out of
ours,
now look at our hands broken and our fingers
crushed underneath boiling rocks.
Hungry Ghosts & the other gimmicks of mortality, they're
coming to roost...

HWÆT, let's abolish the coffee shops & french press the air,
liberate the
caffeine! So that we may never
feel tired again. Next, the thrift stores for our second hands,
and swear an oath to Henry VIII that
we'll sack them like a Welsh monastery but for a gig nay a
gag, instead of iconoclasm
And divorce. They get it all for free anyways. Laugh track.

We'll bleed the tattoo parlors dry just for their ink
and the pensive thought pieces, finally in the rain,
where blotted black lines run wet,
in the puddles where there's no consequence for the
epiphanies
which aren't deep! Why stop there — drag our

picturesque pitchforks to the hipster
grocery stores, break down their self-checkout.
Yes, all the green saints of Vice with their
purple psychiatry, lusting in languish for answers.
Their world's on fire for a moth's heart,
pray for its wings   speak slowly for the Gods,
they've heard it all before.
Their ancient wisdom is at our fingertips,
the ones with tendonitis.
But they hold the Buddha at gunpoint
for a breath.
Hotspurred we begin to harrow our cool blue hell, dissect
our doom, rouse and rotund around a plastic rosary
between our toes, the fingers still broken

ii. Reno

Lake Crowley is where we hung up our high school dreams.
The jet Jeep parked paces away from a fault's grimace in the ground,
from whose iridescent dirt wrote out a poignant script for the night ahead.
Roadtrips are better than the movies and they're best when suddenly stitched
for the express purpose of whimsy. On The Road couldn't have been further

from my mind when spitting stories between aux cord seizures. I hadn't even read
it. We packed that formidable four wheel drive with a carton and a dozen canned
iced tea's. We were commuting dreams and caught in the traffic of crap.

Ignorant, butterfly kisses across the Pacific Time Zone, jettisoned between
sandblasted gift shops and fast food play pens. Wikipedia's article on Occultism
is the snack that held us over between the next interesting drug and subsequent
experimental pop albums. A footballer, two genderqueer punks, and three theater kids
screaming the RENT soundtrack and audibly throwing up across 90s rock playlists.
By the time we got to Reno, the Sun was in Virgo and the moon was full of shit.
Adrenaline and Adore ripped open a stele of Horus across the road, like
eternity's billboard, and suddenly crushed and imploded like a benzodiazepine
under a skateboard, colors on the road became the flavor of life's highways. Love is

a raspberry jammed kiss between friends and debauchery only celebrated
by Dionysus's survivors. After so many tours in the wars of parties, the solace
of an upright back and the twinge of sour candy is the greatest purple heart

iii. Portland

As we watch downtown burn from (the) outside in
the city of Roses a red hot bouquet tonight.
Minister Molotov, did you know
Stalin's granddaughter lives here?
I remember lunch in that city, the one that was meant to be a small town (re: exclusionary)
climbing through a mt hood of pad thai
in the rain
in the sauce
in the charm
like a theme park for the jesters and a Sherwood Forest for the 21st century romantic,
like an exploding heart
tear gas for an appetizer
and a crowd's will unbroken for the side.
Oregon was admitted as a free state to the Union
while denying all the colors of Wimahl

who babbles on like a beautiful baby, for the bicyclists now
for who she
is morning is breakfast is a lazy day off recipe is a titan
is the names they have scurried past is a nun in a wet cloister,
who runs untagged and rapid, like the vans who cross back
on her to whatever unspoken detention center, spraying
gallons of pennyroyal tea into her along the way. Her out of
wedlock children are bullied tangled tabooed and tarnished
This is the only city that can still make a pagan catholic
in its compelling, secondhand dynasties,
          more crete than jerusalem,
less rome than carthage
The crowds cry like a siege of herons on a boggy spring
evening,
they sob cryogenic tears. That is to say, tears for another time
and
they're not performative, they're not to be frozen up to make
snowflakes,
and they're not allergies
but are screams and sirens from the vans of threatening
chrome
unsurprisingly tax exempt.From the wet grimacing boots,
kicking
down on Hawthorne, I'll sneak onto the cheap bus to
Roseburg
                    and hide out there for awhile,

in a Carhartt shirt and rest on the perfect wrists of the
Umpqua River, on the horizon croaks
an estuary of language death towards the North, and a
mouth of rotting teeth

The Cold & Love

Lover, this world is too cold for us.
Blood takes too long to drift down
to the wrist and their rivulet digits.
Bark and branches beat down
our path and eat up the light.

Lover, this world is too cold for us.
Dilly-dally with me, just now.
Smash the screens and leave
them for the condors. We will
return with them, s'mote it be.

Lover, this world is too cold for us.
In your car, we scry for music
and seek in divination, the
perfect mood, an iron to press
into our sternums in travel.

Lover, this world is too cold for us.
We forever chase that warmth,
arms asleep, against each other
for a laurel bough in peace;
a hundred year old robin's nest.

Lover, this world is too cold for us,

and hearts are a curious thing.
Ours will beat together for a little while—
but even as storms of ash and soot,
the winds will carry me off, to find you.

Lover, this world is too cold for us.
From Olympus to Los Angeles,
heart-frostbite makes me restless.
All I need is a few trees, a candle,
one blue blanket and your breasts.

Lover, this world is too cold for us,
and it is cruel in its cold. Frozen
over is Chance and opportunity.
With our pickaxes, we will craft a
new tomorrow, to make fire with ice.

The Economy is Haunted

This whole world is Cæsar
with the walls & the laws,
for there were no saviors in the time of Nero,
just lyres, moaning far cries from the
beloved. The streets are
camera obscuras and the gods,
they're watching, again, from the old houses

It's Babylon or bust. The
Scrabble-headed affair
is a rat's nest with cracked eggs,
the yolk with semen — the Khus
with the Khabs, *anumodana*

Take the best of the world
and you'll see a phoenix
never risen. So many laws
unspoken.

There's no great white North,
but to the sufferings
of the South, an Easterly wind
migrates like broken onion chives,
a rabid stench of the greed of a few
medieval merchants who just wanted

good deals on spices and paper and the
rest of what's known as aisle four.

The petty dreams of Venetian
harbors & Portuguese princes
holds us back like the weight of
porcelain dolls in grandma's
oak hutch from Indiana

Roadkill Rhymes (For The Bodies)

i. a cracked California Condor skull

Life is a game of line breaks where
the syntax trails off and the diction dies
between the clay of words and their goddamn
mortal puzzles. Sore loser I, trapped in the images
I refuse to finish. Monopoly during a summer
evening on a too poor patio table is where
I laid my first critique of capital and still no time
comes to mind where I have won.

Punctuation has never helped or stilled the storms of a
raging,
bowl cut, not even all the apostrophes to the day trips, and
the curious
cadavers we saw along the way:

ii. Raccoon Mother

Flailing across the Palm Desert, where the
wind is pink, where the suburbs' radiation
melts down a little, where the 90's art films and music videos
found a canvas, beat and done.
The sandbitten, maroon(ed) Cadillac in
Aunt Suzie's driveway bears a strong

resemblance to those times, all along the 10
diagonal to Las Vegas, having lost count of
all the sleepy methhead diners with
the catch all arcade machines,

I struggle and sputter to count meter
to myself and others, like in Milton and
his inceled, white lied, cretin thoughts.
But also the rhythms in my own body's
recovery from the poignant posture
that defines my whole generation. Upon
remembering a loitering evening or squatters'
summer, I no longer glaze over the health
of my spine. The body's grammar lies
ill fitting on the pages that try to parse it,

broken images, humor's conjugation

iii. Coyote Father

Anonymous I drive by the vacated duplexes of poetry (credit check required) out easterly,
cornered in on dust laden avenues just outside the dead downtown theory
and pygmy high rises of unwarranted cosmic criticism.
Still, I find no place quite as rich as convenience stores

that never close. The word for the zoning semblances is stretched by and through
our houses divided on lease, confession, tuition, and prestige

a millennium of ivory towers screech
from the ashes of forlorn lineages
titan to olympian. Hermes —
I'll muster the courage to dedicate
myself to you one day.

iv. Opossum Family

Poetry is one hundred unghazalled lines,
all born bastards to gritting syllables for
mothers. The question of raising them is
of the flintrock or cliff, left up to a midwife
from antiquity. She'll seer them to phrase or toss
them to the ether of left behind bed thoughts. For them
to float in these flames, mere scaffolding to a
midrise tower, is to bear feelings in a face.
Such scattered poems will grow up to be like
their fathers: nothing like how their fathers want
themselves to be seen, no less not wanting
to be seen as their fathers. Fathers are poetry

when they inspire so much of it, with crushed
velvet jeers and chicken scratch hugs, always with
the wings to fly fucked off. Amethyst skin after
the curls and hurls of their love, purpled by the
words of unkempt dreams gone fuzzy in the fridge.
These declines into death beget the poems worthy
of no title or glory because they have to be bastards.
Fatherhood is out of the equation. Interpretation, the
final usurping of the throne of dukkha
and the midwife throws oil and ethanol onto a rag and
snuffs us into the Summerland and down the dregs of
ankles
broken and skulls galvanized in pieces twenty down her cliff

with the dregs bulging ink, more our spit or blood,
fishing for the marks of onion chive foamways, the way
watching the shores from the sun's pivot, inheriting
all the memories that the Polaroid hipsters could not
take. The butts of nicotine streams comatose on
the cement liminal, the edgy overture of
long nights spent away from home and further from
the road. There's been no major renovation in
transportation infrastructure since Kerouac and my
peers wonder why Rupi Kaur sells.

v. a peeled away lizard tail

My dearest wish is to be taken back to the water park
outside my hometown where the gods are stuck on their
invisible canals or marinating in the sand. Sometimes these
dreams were forced to die because we cherish them too hard
with the cream of eyes and hands, the cancer of sensation,
the broken lands of touch and experience, their industry
stripping the page of scratches and siphoning all that make a
rose romantic. After the funeral, we can newly purpose
our fleshy vessels into an experience that is less of a chore,
and fashion into a vehicle for transit over a fresh highway,
flying, whooshing and profligating like a head's
weightlessness
as a rollercoaster goer, navigating a trail of enlightened
deserts,
where the body retires in Palm Springs and dresses in pink
button-ups
and the words take a vow of silence in a Veronese villa, all
blown
back by a westerly wind and the servile cracks widened age
and its tender lessons. There is no pain in words:
it is but all they are.

Insufflating Darkness

The park was closed though
without signage nor doors;
still open for business as you were.
I sat with my pack, an unsavory
kind, and my Camels with their
humps at this Wonderland silent
auction. The souls with the tea where
you'd find me in the buttered bread
in the company of sugared blood.
You were deliciously enveloped
in the rhythms of sin
you were just freckles on the
nose of Marcus Aurelius,
you were candy to dead germs
gnashing at dopamine receptors.
These fish hooks were out of
season on a longboat in the
Caribbean. The park at night
was just a vessel for Dionysus,
rituals of dancing olfactorily.
A camel on the shore to wave
you down, silly boat. Our
friendship a harbor: a port
of deaths and entrances,
trade envoys exchanging

sadness for acceptance
and clearance forms from the
lighthouse on the stone beach
I am burning at, Kamel Red in mouth,
watching you and nameless rabbits
insufflate darkness and rattle your skulls
wasted on the shell-less shorelines

An Autumn's Tale

I smoked an opium-hash with you
in a Honda Element, under
the spooky set of stars rife with
umbrellas full of moonwater.

The pipe burnt my hand and
compassion's ladle submerged
my forearm in a slather of anxiolytic
gumbo as I flicked the lighter

like a broken rosary. I am lobotomy
bored of writing about faith. But I
can only birth the gods through my
frontal lobe, the same wrestling mat

where I face the title for a gender.
I couldn't feel my legs that night as
we walked through the pumpkin fields
and the trellises of terror, where hung

a scarecrow ceremoniously wrapped
in the jacket of a forefather, lost in war.
I was as close to him as ever, and ever
will I jar the chutney of your love sweet,

a recipe I cannot pass to the children
we were afraid to have. Down in the
bark by the trellis, a seed of me waits
for an ambitious crow to sow me away

in the next field over, where the town
carnival runs eternal. I — reborn as a
clown, striped like a beatnik and wailing
like a jukebox: *waileway, chumba, wumba*

Sunbleached

Blood orange horizon over beaten blue minivan. The wheels
cauterized
by a road's love. This is how I remember my very first sunrise,
washing the crowning rays down with a fast food breakfast,
silver-dollar sized pancakes and me just as slim, after an
infancy
with the sickly sort of stomach. Syrup, maple in heritage and
co-opted
by corn, emanated and hovered over flapjacks like the
entrails of
one-night-stand of Apollo Phoebus. I knew no better,
nor was I any wiser churned than the store-born butter. A
meal
mass-made for an aesthetic of happiness. Today more than
usual these stars,
the sun's compatriots are deep as they are dead. Their
electric pulses
are paused like the faux poster rotundas of a streaming
service's interface. That medium itself serves as some
electronic eulogy
to video rental stores gone by. Believe it or not they'll stage
the back-
drops of my dreams before the stars do, with plot holes like a
moth-bitten

Bayeux tapestry. Each time, I rewind the river where time's
stinging
nettles weed the threshing floor where one crafts the
unconscious.
So as to say, I carouse the zigzagging and unkempt aisles,
magnetic tape lassoing
the doctored times. There is no polish or VCR head cleaner
that can alleviate time's grain and the rough meal for
the soul it feeds out. Nostalgia in marketing appeals to the
disenfranchised, whose fungi fraught food keep their
hallucinations
of midmorning wishes. Next course, I swallow a memory
after the sword
and leave room for the sweet fatigue of entertainment's
bloody throes.
So maybe tonight, I'll find something to stream. Another
world to rent,
turning my astrolabe away from the constellations of broken
pipes and piss
and towards an orange VHS; filled longingly with predictable
scenes of
pancakes and sunshine rubbing my senses wild like a
midnight
masseuse, stars skinned like potatoes and their shavings
shimmering

A Pantoum to Dark Mother

Death dances daintily in the winds,
I see her sweet bones, sum of white,
The ages, as streets, she walks with wallow,
in decay and darkdusk, sowing seeds of rebirth.
I see her sweet bones, sum of white:
Dull as whispers, soft as skin.
In decay and darkdusk, sowing seeds of rebirth,
in rage, to live and suffer sweetly.
Dull as whispers, soft as skin,
I have known her since I was small.
In rage, to live and suffer sweetly,
A stone before a cave is her abode.
I have known her since I was small.
The ages, though streets, she walks with wallow.
A stone before a cave is her abode,
Death dances daintily in the winds.

New Myth Excerpt

On the day where wind made tea with dead leaves
and blew neither thin nor slack, stirring
some zephyrs of spring, massaging the trunks of
trees licking their limbs, and salivating.
The sun was nooned and our moon tucked in a
bed, a sick child. That day is when the Kosmic Goat, Pan
visited the Lord Buddha: Shakyamuni.

Shakyamuni sat at the foot of a Bodhi tree, twisting his
fingers
in his lap. His half smile, like pollen, blessing the wishes of
another
world onto the blades of grass tickling his feet. The roots the
branches the path — hundreds of human generations trapped
in the caw of the Earth. He sat for them, adjacent to the

swampy fens and ponds with the acrid water, the baths of
lotus blossoms,
the organs of the meadow

Pan, the young and the old, the god and the minstrel, the billy
goat and the shepherd,
he swung with swagger, farting prosody from his pipes,
whistling a tale of the nymph
that got away

and to that, Shakyamuni had a gust of desire strike him down, like the stench of an unearthed grave

"These groves are the harvest
fields of enlightenment. Why
now do you seek to entreat me
away from my practice?"
"I want the seeds beneath us to quiver
and quack like the bushes where
animals hide to make new families. The
trees to heave like an old woman with a
young lover, the flush of a face gone with
the cycle of a new moon."

Lord Buddha gawked at the whirls making his horns, the spirals and scrapes and sutures,
the sex and the soul, coming apart slowly.
Along the corpse of the earth, they sought together but separate
the ways to regenerate the forgotten, fertile spirits of
mother abundance and father virility.
The Goat God and the Awakened One,
their dialogue would not be cast in alabaster.
It would not be coddled in the temples or written on time dried skins,
nor would it end in the manner of pleasantries —
Ovid couldn't care less to inscribe it on a tablet,

and industrialists of the bored steam and smoke,
those who would harness the decrypt flames and
fumes
of one million undead tons,
not on hemp nor carbon nor bleached paper
would the dialogue be recorded on.
Ānanda, their mind nearly omniscient, the crystals
of the ears remained unfettered by the sounds of his Teacher
and the calls of a goat. A band of fairies distracted the
Treasurer
for the afternoon. Animal thoughts have no place on human
parchment.

"You have traveled so far from the West,
my attendants and peers in meditation
have so many wondrous visions emanating
from there. Meadows where lotuses bloom
from the peripheral corner of every eye, walls
of pearls and molten honey, clay mashed from
the dirt of the Devas and blissful tears of Tathagatas
which are crafted holographic and translucent,
like oil muddied puddles of delicate rain,
so as to immediately recognize the mind the
memories the mud
the distortion of illusion, as just blemishes on a
mirror.

Certainly, my dear Pan, is there a kingdom like this in the West?"

Shrieking and ejaculating with deep bellied laughter,
the Kosmic Goat padded the back and brushed the deeply red sanghati
robes of the Prince formerly known as Siddhartha Gautama, still known
as Lord Shakyamuni, a pallbearer in Karma's funeral procession, and a
pair of ears for a lovely, old Goat

"Buddha dear, the Holy and Austere Awakened one", Pan panted,
"I come from a humid, greeny, rocky island where 'lotuses
twinkling in each eye', as you describe, are merely and solely just more islands of a rocky kind and mossy quality, as so many
nymphs, satyrs and for that matter, humans, populate them.
Lord Shakyamuni, I come from fields of grainy food,
vineyards, and threshing floors filled to the brim with semen!
Thumps of desire. The West is not enlightened or beautiful
like how you describe it.

"Each time the muddling men of Athens have a chance

to honor the gods or receive blessings from their emissaries, it is blown back with an artificial inertia; though dandelion spores softly stabbing the eyes of the honest wisher.
Lotus flowers are not found in the agora, Spartan warriors rip them from the ground of their new colonies, and wipe their filthy dicks
with the pink pedals. I worry for the world that not comes now, but generations from the imprints of our steps here, in this grove. Athenian ambition and Spartan strife will make a molten cast for
a man to fill and such a man will fill men and men and further men to be conqueror not of their hearts, but of the trees that engender for us two such a pleasant walk. The Pure Land you dream of during your focused sits under the Bodhi tree, it is already being stomped out"

and the ground tremoured
and the leaves sank
and the deer growled
and Lord Buddha shuttered
looking to the west

Patroclus

Before I had nose-whisked away through all the tone deaf,
broken metrics in paperback translations of the *Iliad* or
Odyssey,
I knew you were my Patroclus. Don't let me exploit you in
just
a few sentences now. Please rip those coins off your eyes and
play slots and slumbersome seances with your last hands.

There's a small garden for you now, churned with finger
painted
rocks, St. Francis statues, faery homes human handcrafted
and the chiming bells from whom I plead for synchronistic
tones.
You can find me on a bench there, ruminating on the rasps
within your throated calls
of a male Siren. I can't remember what you sound like. So I
fill the vacuum with
playlists, Chili Peppers salted throughout. Here, astrally I can
return to a house
party, with that glass, steel and humble patio table and the
simple instruments
in front of us, the beat up Fender with the stickers from KFC
and The Breeders.
Vegetarian and curious, the meat chunks in the sky withheld
themselves.

You were the company of a certain flower, unphased by his
own beauty though tainted by the ungodly weight
of the nuclear family. Disappear again, in the myth's own
meadows and the ponds for time's flora, with lilypads
and regal eggs teeming atop. Here, I carouse through the
pastoral arcade,

where you'd shoot a sign, a text, an autoelegy, put a unicorn
in the stars dimmed, dumbed and darkened. They skip into
battle for us,
like an elementary school play. I can pretend then, that our
friendship was Trojan:
a fruitive creation, an iridescent obsidian stallion, like your
coated, contagious lungs,
for toppling towers towards tidal tears and tourneys!
Addiction is a dialogue
that no oracle can make sense of. Sweet tea, Camel wides,
plastic chairs and stale
beer, under the broken yolk of swallow eggs, secrets sucked
out like salamander venom and spit
out onto crude scribbles in the sands and ocean suds of the
shore on fire.

Our lives shuttled between drunken uncles demanding the
music we couldn't provide.

Churches with padlocks and electric fences with snakes for eyes and knives for arms.
For a few brief hours all that swept by conversation and distractions,
nesting our dreams. Freer now, to crack open onto a perfect cast iron pan of
predetermination. With all the wars fought over spices, we seasoned ourselves
haphazardly, like there wasn't a small bag of oregano at a bodega down the street
the one with a smoke shop next to it, full of black light posters and sword canes,
beside the hookah pens. Evenings of love and mutual enabling
on a genie's last hesitant wish, by whatever interfaith analogy you'd still prefer.

You always knew how to make an exit, that night months later when you ran across
the overpass, you learned to bless the whole Interstate Five, like a scapegoat forgotten
in the garbage dump outside the temple of Banias,
saturating the road with disembodied and suburban relics, when
the asphalt rang with frayed lyre strings from anachronistic

troubadours, fingering a swelling and mesmerizing solo, in a
titanic scale.
A messenger pigeon came to me bearing the news in a
tobacco wrap
the night after, on account of bad traffic. It scurried through a
passenger window,

as I did faint into the wings of shock. From there I was led
upside down, flutes blaring the pitches of denial. I was
dragged
along for a torrid ride down some streams by the Styx.
I used a screwdriver to make a pipe out of a pomegranate
and stuffed it with all I could find. I gave myself up to the
Gods
there and they let me rest on a mattress of leaves until the
Summer came, salting and sun-drying my eyes.

In that golden aged year, I learned that Grief is
a place you go, where you hang out with
dryads with tall tales, dripping off their boughs,
just to fill Apollo's birdbaths with coins at the bottom. I
snuck two
gold doubloons, the ones bespeckling your peppercorn
soulwells,
squinting and shimmering through the spokes of Fortune's
Wheel, off

from the wrong spin cycle where I had been jammed and washed out,
where I put my last, pitiful cry of the eternal boy. Even Pan died, once.

I met you when you were halfway to Hades, you were a cluster of three
flowers on a pyre of youth that time left to bygone rituals of loss, you were
a variant on tragedy, the goatsong that only rolls around only once
a generation, where by an iron age church now overtaken by vines and ivy:
"Et in Arcadia Ego" festers on a pillar by the road. Long gone ages echo

when I whisper the lyrics from my 90's Spotify Daily Mix, driving somewhere
miserably, it is the only entrance I know to the meadow where the scars
are visible, irrigating a pasture where friendship may rise perennially,
just beside the remnants of a forgotten battlefield from antiquity,
where I may raise sheep for counting before sleep, rams that bleat

like boys, in a voice I don't recall, though a mumbled rock
tune
in a soft and manly note, the same tone and timbre of your
tale,
which I mutter to myself too often when I am finally alone

Puck's Nest (Faunalia in July)

At the earlier inklings of a mischievous summer,
help us make a rambunctious rendez-vous past midnight
under the broken streetlight, a joint of an
arboreal cul-de-sac just out of our line of sight.

Break out the hurdy-gurdy, for a funny chorus, one we can
capture
on an old cassette recorder lifted from a thrift store
dumpster. Let the sweet syllables
ramble and ripple in your solar plexus,
harkening back to the time when your youth
learned to weaponize its ramshackled innocence.
Our Earth flushed scarlet in desire for some damned
whimsy!

Next, hop the fence. One after another,
then climb concave down the concrete
river beds
towards those catacombs
filled with graffiti, bats, and a cybergoth haze,
where the twentieth century met its end, in
the expiration of privacy and hypersexualization
of the panopticon.

Curiosity will keep us all born again,
and one day still, all our brain fog shall
shutter to enlightenment's gaze over
the horizon of the Summerland,
where music diffuses like a dice throw
in shuffle sway, carving the paths through
our parties,
we pieces of an eternal dialogue,
seeping in deepening talks all night and day,
where we beheld one another, in witness,
to life's working class buffet; eating with shrimp for fingers,
mistakes dripped in the ruckus and dins
all to decipher alchemy from tomfoolery
and to the Land of Puck
we'll sail away!
Aboard our vessel of light and smoke,
carrying ourselves to send a blessing to
growth's rancor, for fertile compost,

shortly after Fortune will wrestle her wheels
and then we shall plunge to all degrees
cardinal, soon gone from the sacred
trails that we have held in common.

Hold onto our precious nonsense for all time!
Let it break brightly through your pupils to

save room for us in your glassy eyes' twinkle,
for a graceful aging, and your final sugar tears.

Alice Fulmer

Alice Fulmer (she/her) is a contemporary poet and medieval scholar based in California. She is currently pursuing a PhD in English at University of California, Santa Barbara. In 2020, she received an Honorable Mention from Academy of American Poets for a small manuscript. Find her nowadays reading in bed, with a cat named Precious.

RITONA

RITONA is an imprint of Ritona a.s.b.l., a non-profit publishing organisation advocating for pluralism, tolerance,and respect for Pagan, Indigenous, and non-industrial ways of being in the World.

You can find out more about our work or peruse our many other titles at ABeautifulResistance.com.

www.ingramcontent.com/pod-product-compliance
Ingram Content Group UK Ltd.
Pitfield, Milton Keynes, MK11 3LW, UK
UKHW022007190726
13853UKWH00004B/1783

9 798985 202885